"There is no such thing as *having read* the Bhagavad Gita. You are either reading it, or you are not."

Ramakinananda

As a metaphor for the war within ourselves, the dialogue comprising the world's most famous poem is a conversation between the warrior-prince Arjuna and his charioteer Krishna (a symbolic embodiment of God) in the middle of a great civil war.

For simplified legibility, the dozens of nicknames for each character have been replaced by the consistent use of Arjuna and Krishna. Parentheticals are also used for additional clarification.

Though it is a simple (30 minute) read, it is not an easy read. Like many ancient texts, it is not meant to be read for information, but for transformation; with reflection more important than the reading itself. And that is why deep inquiry would benefit from commentary and explanation by a lifelong scholar and teacher. The compiler of this pocket Gita recommends Swami Parthasarathy's commentary for a comprehensive explanation of this thought-provoking and timeless text.

no nicknames

bhagavad gita

ISBN: 979-8-218-30249-8 (Paperback)

ISBN: 979-8-218-30250-4 (eBook)

Contents

1.

THE YOGA OF ARJUNA'S DESPONDENCY

1.1   Dhṛtarāṣṭra (king of the unrighteous army, enemy
        of Arjuna) said:

        Assembled on the sacred field of Kurukṣetra,
        desirous to fight, what did the sons of Pāṇḍu
        (Arjuna's family) and mine do, O Sañjaya (his
        advisor with the power to see happenings far
        away)?

1.2   Sanjaya (giving context in this chapter with several
        names that are not critical to know about; the
        philosophy begins at verse 20 of this chapter)
        said: Indeed, having seen the army of the
        Pāṇḍavas arrayed in battle, King Duryodhana then
        approached the teacher and spoke (these) words.

1.3   Behold, O teacher, this mighty army of the sons of
        Pāṇḍu arrayed for battle by the son of Drupada,
        your wise pupil.

1.4   Here are heroes, mighty archers, equal in battle to
        Bhīma and Arjuna — Yuyudhāna, Virāṭa and the
        Mahāratha (great chariot-warrior) Drupada.

1.5   Dhṛṣṭaketu, Cekitāna and the valiant king of Kāśi,
        Purujit, Kuntibhoja and Śaibya, the best of men.

1.6   And mighty Yudhāmanyu and brave Uttamaujā,
        Saubhadra and Draupadeyāḥ — all indeed
        mahārathas (great chariot-warriors).

1.7   O Dhṛtarāṣṭra, know also those who are
        distinguished among us, the leaders of my army;
        these I mention to you for information.

1.8 Thyself and Bhīṣma and Karṇa and Kṛpa, the victorious in battle; Aśvatthāmā, Vikarṇa and also the son of Somadatta.

1.9 And many other heroes who have given up their lives for my sake, armed with various weapons and missiles, all well-skilled in battle.

1.10 This army of ours (the unrighteous army), protected by Bhīṣma is unlimited, whereas that army of theirs (the righteous army) protected by Bhīma is limited.

1.11 And stationed in your respective positions in all divisions, all of you guard Bhīṣma alone.

1.12 The mighty grandsire, the aged Kuru, raising aloud a lion's roar blew his conch to cheer him up.

1.13 Then conches, kettledrums, tabors, drums and cowhorns blared forth quite suddenly; that noise was tumultuous.

1.14 Then, seated in a magnificent chariot yoked to white horses, Krishna and Arjuna also blew their divine conches.

1.15 Krishna blew the Pāñcajanya, Arjuna, the Devadatta and Vṛkodara of terrible deeds, the great conch Pauṇḍra.

1.16 King Yudhiṣṭhira, son of Kunti, (blew) Anan-tavijaya and Nakula and Sahadeva, Sughoṣa and Maṇipuṣpaka.

1.17   And Kāśya (king of Kāśi), an excellent archer, and
        śikhaṇḍī, a mahāratha (great chariot-warrior),
        Dhṛṣṭadyumna and Virāûa and the invincible
        Sātyaki.

1.18   O Lord of earth, Drupada and the sons of Draupadī
        and the mighty-armed son of Subhadrā, all of them
        blew their respective conches.

1.19   These tumultuous sounds rent the hearts of
        Dhṛtarāṣṭra's host and made earth and sky
        reverberate.

1.20   Then seeing Dhṛtarāṣṭra's host standing arrayed
        ready to operate the weapons, Arjuna, with the
        monkey ensign, taking up his bow said these words
        to Krishna, the Lord of Earth.

1.21-1.22 Arjuna said: Place my chariot between the two
        armies, O Krishna, that I may see these standing
        desirous to fight, with whom all I must fight in this
        outbreaking battle.

1.23   I observe those who are assembled here to fight
        wishing to please in battle the evil-minded son of
        Dhṛtarāṣṭra (Duryodhana, Arjuna's evil-minded
        parallel warrior prince and son of King Dhṛtarāṣṭra).

1.24   Thus addressed by Arjuna, Krishna, having drawn
        up the best of chariots between the two armies.

1.25   In front of Bhīṣma, Droṇā and all the rulers of the
        earth said, "O Arjuna, behold these Kurus gathered
        together."

1.26   There Arjuna saw standing fathers, grandfathers,
       teachers, maternal uncles, brothers, sons,
       grandsons and comrades, fathers-in-law and
       friends also in both the armies.

1.27   He, the son of Kuntī, seeing all these kinsmen
       thus standing, filled with deep pity, uttered this in
       sorrow.

1.28-1.29 Arjuna said: Seeing these, O Krishna, one's own
       kinsmen arrayed, desirous to fight, my limbs fail
       and my mouth is parched, my body trembles and
       my hair stands on end.

1.30   Gāṇḍīva slips from my hand and my skin burns all
       over, my mind whirls as it were, and I am not able
       to stand.

1.31   And I see adverse omens, O Keśava, I do not
       foresee any good in killing one's own kinsmen in
       battle.

1.32   I desire not victory O Krishna, nor kingdom nor
       pleasures. Of what avail is kingdom to us, O
       Krishna? Of what avail are enjoyments or life?

1.33   Those for whose sake we desire kingdom,
       enjoyments and pleasures, they stand here in
       battle, having renounced their lives and riches.

1.34   Teachers, fathers, sons, and also grandfathers,
       maternal uncles, fathers-in-law, grandsons,
       brothers-in-law and kinsmen.

1.35   These I do not wish to kill though killed by them,
        O Krishna, even for the sovereignty of the three
        worlds, how then for the earth!

1.36   What pleasure is there in slaying the sons of
        Dhṛtarāṣṭra, O Krishna? Sin alone will accrue to us
        by killing these desperate ones.

1.37   Therefore it does not behove us to kill the sons of
        Dhṛtarāṣṭra, our relatives; for how can we be happy
        by killing our own kinsmen, O charioteer?

1.38   Although these, with intelligence overwhelmed by
        greed, see no evil in the destruction of the family
        and sin in treachery to friends.

1.39   Krishna, why should not we, who clearly see evil
        in the destruction of the family, learn to turn away
        from this sin.

1.40   In the destruction of a family the immemorial
        religious rites of the family perish; having lost
        spirituality, impiety indeed overcomes the entire
        family.

1.41   By the prevalence of impiety, O Krishna, the
        women of the family become corrupt; women
        being corrupted, O Krishna, there arises
        intermixture (of cultures).

1.42   Confusion (of cultures), indeed, leads the
        destroyers-of-family and the family to hell; verily
        their ancestors fall, deprived of the offerings of
        rice-ball and water.

1.43 By these misdeeds of the destroyers-of-family that
      cause intermixture of castes, the eternal religious
      rites of castes and families are destroyed.

1.44 We have heard, O Krishna, that men who have
      lost their family religious rites dwell in hell for an
      indefinite period.

1.45 Alas! We are involved indeed to commit a great sin
      by preparing to slay our own kinsmen for the greed
      of pleasure of kingdom.

1.46 If the sons of Dhṛtarāṣṭra armed with weapons
      should slay me unarmed and unresisting in battle
      that would be better for me.

1.47 Sañjaya (the observer of this conversation and
      the narrator of the Gita to King Dhṛtarāṣṭra) said:
      Having spoken thus in the battlefield, Arjuna sat
      down in the seat of the chariot casting away his
      bow and arrow, with mind distressed in sorrow.

2.

THE YOGA OF KNOWLEDGE

2.1   Sañjaya said: To him who was thus overcome with pity, whose eyes were filled with tears, who was agitated and despondent, Krishna spoke these words.

2.2   The blessed Lord, Krishna (Arjuna's, friend, charioteer, and advisor) said: Whence has this dejection come upon you in a crisis, unworthy of an Āryan, attaining neither heaven nor fame, O Arjuna.

2.3   Yield not to unbecomingness, O Arjuna, it does not befit you. Casting off this mean weakness of heart, arise, O Arjuna.

2.4   Arjuna said: How shall I, O Krishna, fight with arrows against Bhīṣma and Droṇa in battle, they who are worthy of worship, O Krishna?

2.5   Better indeed is to live on alms in this world than to slay the most noble teachers; by slaying them all my enjoyments of wealth and desires even here will be stained with blood.

2.6   Nor do we know which is better for us, that we should conquer them or they should conquer us. The very sons of Dhṛtarāṣṭra, whom having slain we do not wish to live, stand facing us.

2.7   My nature is overpowered by the taint of pity. With my mind confused as to duty I ask thee: Tell me decisively which is good for me. I am thy disciple. Instruct me, who has taken refuge in thee.

2.8   I do not see that which can remove the grief which is drying up my senses even on obtaining prosperous and unrivalled kingdom on earth and lordship over the gods.

2.9   Sañjaya said: Having spoken thus to Krishna, Arjuna, the destroyer of foes, said to Krishna, I will not fight and became silent.

2.10   To him who was despondent in the midst of the two armies, Krishna, smiling, spoke these words.

2.11   The blessed Lord said: You have been grieving for those that should not be grieved for and you speak words of wisdom. The wise grieve neither for the living nor for the dead.

2.12   Never indeed was I not, nor you, nor these rulers of men; also none of us will cease to be hereafter.

2.13   Just as the embodied (passes through) childhood, youth and old age in this body, so does it pass into another body; there the wise one is not grieved.

2.14   The sense contacts, O Arjuna, which cause heat and cold, pleasure and pain, they come and go, they are impermanent; endure them, O Arjuna.

2.15   The person whom, verily, these afflict not, O Arjuna; balanced in pain and pleasure, steadfast, they are fit for immortality.

2.16   The unreal has no existence, the real never ceases to be, the truth about both of these indeed has been seen by the seers of Truth.

2.17 Know indeed That to be indestructible by which all
this is pervaded, none can cause the destruction of
this Imperishable.

2.18 These bodies of the Embodied, which is eternal,
indestructible, immeasurable, are said to have an
end. Therefore fight, O Arjuna.

2.19 He who regards This as slayer, and he who thinks
This is slain, both of them are ignorant. This neither
slays nor is slain.

2.20 This is not born nor does It die, nor having been,
will ever again cease to be; This is unborn, eternal,
changeless, ancient, It is not killed when the body
is killed.

2.21 He who knows This to be indestructible, eternal,
unborn, immutable, how can that person, O
Arjuna, slay anyone or cause anyone to be slain?

2.22 Just as a person casting off worn-out garments puts
on new ones so the embodied, casting off worn-
out bodies, enters new ones.

2.23 Weapons do not cleave This, nor fire burns This,
nor water wets This, nor wind dries.

2.24 This cannot be cut, nor burnt, nor wetted, nor
dried. This is eternal, all-pervading, stable,
immovable and ancient.

2.25 This is said to be unmanifest, This is inconceivable,
This is unchangeable; therefore, knowing This as
such, you should not grieve.

2.26   But if you think This as constantly being born and constantly dying, even then, O Arjuna, you should not grieve like this.

2.27   Certain, indeed, is death for the born and certain is birth for the dead; therefore you should not grieve over the inevitable.

2.28   Beings are unmanifest in their origin, manifest in their middle, unmanifest again in their end, O Arjuna, what is there to grieve about?

2.29   One sees This as a wonder so also another speaks of This as a wonder, another hears of This as a wonder; and though having heard, none knows This at all.

2.30   This Indweller in the bodies of all is ever indestructible, O Arjuna; therefore you should not grieve for any creature.

2.31   Further, looking at your own duty you should not waver, for there is nothing better for a kṣatriya (warrior) than a righteous war.

2.32   Happy are the kṣatriyas, O Arjuna, who get such a battle that comes unsought as an open door to heaven.

2.33   Now, if you will not wage this righteous war, then having abandoned your duty and fame you will incur sin (agitation).

2.34   People also will recount your perpetual dishonor, and to the honored, dishonor is worse than death.

2.35 The great chariot-warriors will think that you have withdrawn from the battle out of fear, and you, that were highly esteemed by them, will be lightly held.

2.36 And your enemies will say many unbecoming words cavilling your prowess. What indeed could be more painful than that?

2.37 Either slain you will attain heaven, or victorious you will enjoy the earth, therefore arise, O Arjuna, determined to fight.

2.38 Treating alike pleasure and pain, gain and loss, victory and defeat, then get ready for battle, thus you will not incur sin (agitation).

2.39 This is the wisdom of sāṅkhya (ancient philosophy) taught to you, now listen to the wisdom of yoga, endowed with which, O Arjuna, you shall cast off the bond of action.

2.40 In this there is no loss of effort nor is there production of contrary result. Even very little of this discipline protects one from great fear.

2.41 In this the intellect is resolute and one-pointed, O Arjuna; many-branched and endless indeed are the thoughts of the irresolute.

2.42 The unwise utter flowery speech, rejoicing in the letter of the Vedas, O Arjuna, saying, There is nothing else than this.

2.43 Obsessed with desires, with heaven as the ultimate goal of birth and action, they prescribe many specific rites for attainment of pleasure and power.

2.44 Those who are attached to pleasure and power (peace and prosperity), whose minds are drawn away by that (flowery speech), have no determined intellect fixed in samādhi (in liberation).

2.45 The Vedas deal with the three guṇas (attributes). Be thou free, O Arjuna, from the three guṇas, free from the pairs of opposites, remain ever in sattva (purity), free from acquisition and preservation and established in the Self.

2.46 To an enlightened Brāhmaṇa, all the Vedas are of as much use as a pond is where there is a flood of water everywhere.

2.47 Your right is in action only, never to the fruits; let not the fruit of action be your motive nor let your attachment be to inaction.

2.48 Steadfast in yoga, perform actions O Arjuna, renouncing attachment and being the same in success and failure; this evenness is called yoga.

2.49 Far inferior to yoga of knowledge is action, O Arjuna. Seek refuge in knowledge; wretched are they whose motive is fruit.

2.50 United to knowledge, one sheds here both good and bad deeds, therefore devote yourself to yoga; skill in action is yoga.

2.51 The wise, united to knowledge, renouncing the fruit of action, liberated from the bond of birth, indeed reach the state beyond evil.

2.52 When your intellect will cross the mire of delusion then you will grow indifferent to what has been heard and what is yet to be heard.

2.53 When your intellect, perplexed by what has been heard, shall stand immovable and steady in meditation then you will attain yoga (union, Self-realization, God-consciousness, liberation).

2.54 Arjuna said: What is the description of one of steady wisdom merged in the super-conscious state, O Krishna? How does one of steady wisdom speak, how does one sit, how does one walk?

2.55 The blessed Lord said: *When one completely casts off all desires of the mind and is satisfied in the Self, by the Self*, O Arjuna, then is one said to be of steady wisdom.

2.56 He whose mind is not agitated by sorrow nor excited by joy, who is free from desire, fear and anger, they are called sages of steady wisdom.

2.57 He who is everywhere without attachment, who having met good or evil neither rejoices nor hates, his wisdom is established.

2.58 When, like the tortoise drawing in its limbs on all sides, he withdraws his senses from sense objects, then his wisdom is established.

2.59   The sense objects turn away from an abstinent
        man but not the relish (the taste for them);
        but even his relish turns away upon seeing the
        Supreme.

2.60   O Arjuna, the turbulent senses of even a wise man
        while striving, indeed forcibly carry away his mind.

2.61   Having controlled them all, he should sit focussed
        on Me, the Lord, as supreme. His wisdom is
        established indeed whose senses are under
        control.

2.62   A man musing on objects develops attachment for
        them, from attachment arises desire, from desire
        arises anger. The ladder of fall.

2.63   From anger arises delusion, from delusion
        confusion of memory, from confusion of memory
        loss of intellect, from loss of intellect, he perishes.

2.64   But the self-controlled man, free from likes and
        dislikes, moving among objects with his senses
        under control attains peace.

2.65   In peace all his sorrows are destroyed, the intellect
        of the tranquil-minded soon becomes steady.

2.66   There is neither knowledge nor meditation for
        the unsteady, and to the unmeditative, there is
        no peace; to the peaceless, how can there be
        happiness?

2.67   For the mind, which follows the roving senses,
carries away his intellect as the wind carries away a
boat on water.

2.68   Therefore, O Arjuna, his wisdom is established
whose senses are completely restrained from
sense objects.

2.69   That which is night to all beings, therein the self-
controlled one keeps awake; that in which beings
are awake is night to the sage who *sees*.

2.70   As the waters enter the ocean, which filled from all
sides, remains undisturbed, likewise, he in whom
all objects of enjoyment enter, attains peace — not
the desirer of objects.

2.71   That person, *who abandons all desires and moves
about without yearning, and without the sense of
'I' and 'mine'*, they attain peace.

2.72   This is the state of Brahman, O Arjuna; attaining
this, none is deluded. Being established therein,
even at the end of life, one attains oneness with
Brahman (God).

3.

THE YOGA OF ACTION

3.1   O Krishna, if you consider knowledge superior to
        action, why then do you, O Krishna, engage me in
        terrible action?

3.2   With an apparently perplexing speech, you confuse
        my understanding; tell me with certainty the one
        (way) by which I may attain the highest.

3.3   Krishna said: In this world there is a two-fold path,
        as I said before O Arjuna — the path of knowledge
        for the sāṅkhyas (contemplative) and the path of
        action for the yogīs (active).

3.4   Not by abstaining from action does man gain
        actionlessness, nor by mere renunciation does he
        attain Perfection.

3.5   None can ever remain inactive even for a moment;
        all are made to act helplessly indeed by the
        qualities born of prakṛti (nature).

3.6   He who, restraining the organs of action, sits
        mentally indulging in the sense objects, he, of
        deluded understanding, is called a hypocrite.

3.7   But he who restraining the senses by the mind, O
        Arjuna, engages his organs of action in the yoga of
        action, without attachment, he excels.

3.8   Perform your obligatory action, for action is
        superior to inaction; and even the maintenance of
        your body would not be possible by inaction.

3.9   This world is bound by action other than those
        performed for the sake of yajña (sacrifice), O

Arjuna. Perform action for that sake, free from attachment.

3.10   The Creator, having in the beginning created mankind together with yajña (sacrifice), said, "By this shall you propagate, let this be the milk-cow of your desired objects."

3.11   Nourish the gods with this, and may those gods nourish you; nourishing one another, you shall attain the Supreme good.

3.12   Verily, the gods, nourished by sacrifice, will give you the desired enjoyments. He who enjoys what is given by them without having offered to them, is indeed a thief.

3.13   The righteous who eat the remnants of sacrifice are freed from all sins (agitations), but those sinners (agitated agitators), who cook for their own sake, eat sin (agitation).

3.14   From food, come forth beings, from rain, food is produced, from yajña (sacrifice), arises rain and yajña (sacrifice) is born of action.

3.15   Know that action arises from Brahmā, and Brahmā arises from the Imperishable. Therefore, the all-pervading Brahman (God) ever rests in yajña (sacrifice).

3.16   He who does not follow here, the wheel thus set in motion, living in agitation and rejoicing in the senses, he lives in vain, O Arjuna.

3.17   *But the one who rejoices in the Self, is satisfied in the Self and is content in the Self alone, for him, there is nothing to be done.*

3.18   For him there is no interest whatever here in what is done or what is not done, nor does he depend upon any being for any object.

3.19   Therefore, without attachment always perform actions which should be done, for by performing action without attachment man reaches the Supreme.

3.20   Verily by action alone Janaka and others attained Perfection; even with an eye to the welfare of the world, also you should perform action.

3.21   Whatsoever the superior person does, that alone other people do, whatever standard he sets, that standard the world follows.

3.22   O Arjuna, there is nothing in the three worlds that has to be done by Me, nor anything unattained that has to be attained, yet I engage in action.

3.23   If indeed even I do not ever engage in action, unwearied, men would in every way follow my path, O Arjuna.

3.24   These worlds would perish if I did not perform action. I should be the cause of confusion of castes and should destroy these people.

3.25 O Arjuna, as the ignorant act, attached to action, so should the wise one act, unattached, wishing the welfare of the world.

3.26 Let not the wise man unsettle the minds of the ignorant attached to action; *acting united (with the Self) let him render all actions attractive.*

3.27 Actions in all cases are performed by the guṇas (qualities) of prakṛti (nature); one who is deluded by egoism thinks "I am the doer."

3.28 But he, O Arjuna, with true insight into the distinctions of guṇas (qualities) and actions, knowing that guṇas (as senses) abide in guṇas (as objects), is not attached.

3.29 Those deluded by the guṇas (qualities) of prakṛti (nature) are attached to the functions of the guṇas; the one of perfect knowledge should not unsettle the dull-witted whose knowledge is imperfect.

3.30 Renouncing all actions in Me, with thoughts resting on the Self, free from hope and attachment, fight without mental fever.

3.31 Those men who constantly practice this teaching of Mine, full of śraddhā (determined faith) and without petty objection, they too are liberated from actions.

3.32 But those who carp at this teaching of Mine and do not practice it, deluded in all knowledge and senseless, know them to be ruined.

3.33   Even a man of knowledge acts in accordance with his own nature; beings follow their nature, what can restraint do?

3.34   Attachment and aversion for the objects of the senses abide in the senses; let none come under the dominion of these two for they are one's enemies.

3.35   Better is svadharma (one's own duty) though devoid of merit than paradharma (duty of another) well discharged; better is death in svadharma, *paradharma is fraught with fear.*

3.36   Arjuna said: But by what impelled does man commit sin though against his wish O Krishna, constrained as it were by force?

3.37   The blessed Lord said: It is desire, it is anger, born of the quality of rajas (mental fever), all-devouring, all-sinful; know this to be the foe here.

3.38   As fire is covered by smoke, as a mirror by dust, as an unborn child is covered by the womb, so is This covered by it.

3.39   O Arjuna, wisdom is covered by this constant enemy of the wise in the form of desire, as insatiable fire.

3.40   The senses, mind, and intellect are said to be its seat; veiling wisdom through these, it deludes the embodied.

3.41   Therefore, O Arjuna, controlling first the senses, indeed, kill this sinful destroyer of knowledge and wisdom.

3.42   The senses are said to be great, greater than the senses is the mind, greater than the mind is the intellect; that which is greater than the intellect is God.

3.43   Thus knowing that which is greater than the intellect and restraining the self by the self, O Arjuna, kill the enemy in the form of desire, hard to conquer.

4.

THE YOGA OF RENUNCIATION OF ACTION IN WISDOM

4.1   The blessed Lord said: I declared this imperishable yoga to Vivasvān, Vivasvān taught it to Manu, Manu taught it to Ikṣvāku.

4.2   Thus handed down in succession, the king-sages knew this; this yoga, by long lapse of time, has been lost here, O Arjuna.

4.3   That same ancient yoga has today been imparted to you by Me for you are my devotee and friend, and this indeed is the Supreme secret.

4.4   Arjuna said: Later was your birth, earlier the birth of Vivasvān; how then am I to understand that you taught this in the beginning.

4.5   The blessed Lord said: Many births of mine and yours have passed by, O Arjuna; I know them all while you know not, O Arjuna.

4.6   Though unborn, of imperishable nature and Lord of beings, presiding over my own prakṛti (matter, nature) I am born by my own māyā (power, illusion).

4.7   O Arjuna, whenever there is indeed a decline of dharma (righteousness) and a rise of adharma (unrighteousness), then I manifest Myself.

4.8   For the protection of the virtuous, for the destruction of the wicked, and for the establishment of dharma (righteousness), I am born from age to age.

4.9   He who knows thus my divine birth and action in
true light, having abandoned the body, is not born
again; he comes to Me, O Arjuna.

4.10   Freed from desire, fear and anger, absorbed in
Me, taking refuge in Me, purified by the fire of
knowledge, many have attained my Being.

4.11   Howsoever men approach Me, even so do I satisfy
them; men tread My path in all ways, O Arjuna.

4.12   They, who long for success in action here, sacrifice
to the gods, for quickly indeed success is born of
action in the human world.

4.13   The four-fold caste was created by Me according
to the differentiation of guṇa (quality) and action;
though I am its author, know Me to be the non-
doer and immutable.

4.14   Actions do not taint Me, nor have I a desire for the
fruit of action; he who knows Me thus is not bound
by actions.

4.15   Having known thus, action was performed even
by the ancient seekers of liberation; therefore you
also perform action as the ancients did in olden
times.

4.16   Even the wise are deluded here as to what is action
and what is inaction; therefore, I shall teach you
action, knowing which, you will be liberated from
evil.

| 4.17 | Verily action should be known, and forbidden action also should be known, and inaction should be known; the nature of action is impenetrable. |

4.18 He, who sees inaction in action and action in inaction, is wise among men; he is a yogī, a doer of all actions.

4.19 He whose undertakings are free from desire and expectation, whose actions are burnt by the fire of knowledge, him the wise call a sage.

4.20 Having renounced attachment to fruit of action, ever content, depending on nothing, he does not do anything, though he is engaged in action.

4.21 Hoping for naught, with mind and body controlled, having relinquished all possessions, doing mere bodily action, he incurs no sin.

4.22 Content with whatever is got unsought, rising above the pairs of opposites, free from envy, equanimous in success and failure, though acting, he is not bound.

4.23 One who is devoid of attachment, liberated, with mind established in knowledge, acting for yajña (sacrifice), his whole action is dissolved.

4.24 The act of offering is Brahman, the oblation is Brahman, offered by Brahman in the fire of Brahman, by seeing Brahman in action, Brahman verily shall be reached by him.

4.25   Some yogīs perform sacrifice to gods; others perform sacrifice by offering sacrifice itself in the fire of Brahman.

4.26   Others offer hearing and other senses as sacrifice into the fires of restraint; others offer sound and other sense objects as sacrifice in the fires of the senses.

4.27   Others sacrifice all the functions of the senses and the functions of the vital-airs into the fire of yoga of self-control, kindled by wisdom.

4.28   Yet others again offer wealth as sacrifice, austerity as sacrifice, yoga as sacrifice and ascetics of rigid vows offer study and wisdom as sacrifice.

4.29   Yet others offer as sacrifice prāṇa (incoming breath) into apāna (outgoing breath) and apāna into prāṇa; restraining the courses of prāṇa and apāna, some are absorbed in prāṇāyāma (breath control).

4.30   Others, with regulated food, offer prāṇas (life-breaths) into prāṇas (life-breaths). All these are knowers of sacrifice and by sacrifice have destroyed their sins.

4.31   Eaters of the nectar, the remnant of sacrifice, go to the eternal Brahman. This world is not for the non-sacrificer, how then the other, O Arjuna?

4.32 Thus manifold sacrifices are spread out before Brahman. Know them all to be born of action; thus knowing, you shall be liberated.

4.33 The sacrifice-of-wisdom is superior to the sacrifice-of-wealth, O Arjuna. All actions without exception, O Arjuna, culminate in wisdom.

4.34 Know that by prostration, by questioning, and by service, the wise who have realized the Truth will teach you the knowledge.

4.35 Knowing which you shall not again get deluded thus, O Arjuna, by which you will see all beings in the Self, also in Me.

4.36 Even if you are the most sinful of all sinners, you shall verily cross over all sin by the *raft of knowledge.*

4.37 As blazing fire reduces fuel to ashes, O Arjuna, so does the fire of knowledge reduce all actions to ashes.

4.38 *Verily, there is no purifier here like knowledge; he who is perfected in yoga finds it in the Self in time.*

4.39 He who has śraddhā (determined faith), who is devoted, who has subdued the senses attains knowledge, having attained knowledge he ere long gains supreme Peace.

4.40 The ignorant, devoid of śraddhā (determined faith), the doubting-self is ruined; there is neither this world, nor the other nor happiness for the doubting-self.

4.41   He who has renounced actions by yoga, whose doubts are rent asunder by knowledge, who is poised in the Self, actions do not bind him, O Arjuna.

4.42   *Therefore cutting asunder with the sword of knowledge this ignorance-born doubt of the Self, dwelling in your heart, be established in yoga. Arise, O Arjuna!*

5.

THE YOGA OF RENUNCIATION IN ACTION

5.1   Arjuna said: O Krishna, you praise renunciation of action and again yoga (path of action); tell me conclusively which of the two is better.

5.2   The blessed Lord said: Both renunciation and yoga of action lead to supreme Bliss; but of the two, yoga of action is superior to renunciation of action.

5.3   He should be known as a perpetual sannyāsī (ascetic) who neither hates nor desires; for, free from the pairs of opposites, O Arjuna, he is easily set free from bondage.

5.4   Children, not the wise, speak of sāṅkhya (contemplation and philosophy) and yoga (action and union) as different; he who is duly established in one obtains the fruit of both.

5.5   That state which is reached by the sāñkhyas is reached by the yogīs also; he who sees sāṅkhya (contemplation) and yoga (action) as one, he sees.

5.6   But *renunciation, O Arjuna, is hard to attain without yoga (action);* a sage, well established in yoga, attains Brahman ere long.

5.7   He who is united by yoga, who has purified and conquered the self, subdued his senses, *who realizes his Self as the Self in all beings*, is not tainted, although acting.

5.8   The knower of Truth, united with Self, thinks I do nothing at all: seeing, hearing, touching, smelling, eating, going, sleeping, breathing—

5.9   Speaking, releasing, seizing, opening and closing the eyes — he is convinced, "The senses move among the sense objects."

5.10   He who, dedicating his actions to Brahman, acts abandoning attachment, is not tainted by sin as a lotus leaf (is not tainted) by water.

5.11   The yogīs, having abandoned attachment, perform action merely by the senses, body, mind, and intellect for self-purification.

5.12   The yukta (united one) having abandoned the fruit of action, attains eternal peace, the ayukta (non-united), impelled by desire and attached to fruit, is bound.

5.13   Mentally renouncing all actions and self-controlled, the embodied rests happily in the city of nine gates (the physical body), neither even acting nor causing to act.

5.14   The Lord creates neither doership nor actions nor the union with fruit of action for the world; but nature manifests itself.

5.15   The Lord accepts neither the sin nor even the virtue of anyone; knowledge is veiled by ignorance, beings are thereby deluded.

5.16   But in whom ignorance is destroyed by knowledge, in them knowledge reveals the Supreme like the sun.

5.17   With mind and intellect established in That, with
       That as the supreme goal, they, whose sins have
       been dispelled by knowledge, reach a state of no
       return.

5.18   The wise view equally a brāhmaṇa endowed with
       learning and humility, a cow, an elephant, a dog
       and even an outcaste (one outside all castes).

5.19   Even here, birth is overcome by those whose
       mind rests in evenness; Brahman (God) is indeed
       spotless and equal, therefore they are established
       in Brahman.

5.20   With steady intellect established in Brahman, the
       undeluded knower of Brahman neither rejoices on
       obtaining what is pleasant nor grieves on obtaining
       what is unpleasant.

5.21   Unattached to external contacts one finds the
       happiness that is in the Self; uniting oneself to
       Brahman by yoga, one attains eternal bliss.

5.22   For, *the enjoyments that are born of senses are
       only wombs of sorrow*; they have a beginning and
       an end. O Arjuna, the wise one does not rejoice in
       them.

5.23   He who is able to withstand even here, before
       liberation from the body, the force arising from
       desire and anger, he is a yogī, he is a happy man.

5.24   He or she who is happy within, who rejoices within, who is illumined within, that yogī alone, becoming Brahman, gains the bliss of Brahman.

5.25   Sages attain the bliss of Brahman whose sins have been destroyed, whose dualities are destroyed, who are self-controlled, who revel in the welfare of all beings.

5.26   *For those who are freed from desire and anger, who are self-controlled, who have subdued their mind completely, who have realized the Self, the bliss of Brahman resides in them.*

5.27   Shutting out external senses and fixing the gaze as though between the eyebrows, equalizing the flow of incoming and outgoing breaths in the nostrils.

5.28   Having the senses, mind, and intellect controlled, with liberation as the goal, the sage, free from desire, anger and fear, is verily liberated forever.

5.29   Having known Me as the enjoyer of sacrifices and austerities, the supreme Lord of all worlds, the friend of all beings, he attains peace.

6.

YOGA OF MEDITATION

6.1   The blessed Lord said: He who does his bounden
       duty without depending on the fruit of action, he is
       a sannyāsī (ascetic, contemplator, philosopher) and
       a yogī (one seeking union); *not the one without fire
       and not the one without action.*

6.2   O Arjuna, know yoga to be that which they call as
       sannyāsa (contemplator); none indeed becomes a
       yogī without renouncing saṅkalpa (thoughts).

6.3   For a seeker who wishes to master yoga, action
       is said to be the means; for the one who is
       established in yoga, quietude is said to be the
       means.

6.4   When a man is not attached, either to sense
       objects or actions, and has renounced all thoughts,
       then he is said to be established in yoga.

6.5   Let man lift himself by himself, let him not lower
       himself; his self alone is his friend, his self alone is
       his enemy.

6.6   *For him who has conquered his self, the Self is his
       friend but for him who has not conquered his self,
       the Self verily becomes hostile like an enemy.*

6.7   *The supreme One, who is self-controlled and
       peaceful, is balanced in cold and heat, in pleasure
       and pain, as also in honour and dishonour.*

6.8   *The yogī, who is satisfied with knowledge and
       wisdom, who remains unshaken, who has
       conquered the senses, to whom a lump of earth,*

stone, and gold are the same, is said to be a realized One.

6.9 *He who has equal regard for the good-hearted, friends, foes, indifferent, neutral, hateful, relatives, righteous and unrighteous, he excels.*

6.10 Let the yogī remaining in solitude, alone, seated, with mind and body controlled, constantly practicing union with the Self, free from desire and possession.

6.11 Having established in a clean place a firm seat of his own, neither too high nor too low, with cloth, skin and kuśa grass thereon.

6.12 There, having made the mind one-pointed, with the functions of the mind and senses controlled, seated on the seat, let him practice yoga for self-purification.

6.13 Holding body, head, and neck erect, still and firm, gazing at the tip of the nose and not looking around.

6.14 Serene-minded, fearless, firm in the vow of brahmacharya (self-control), the mind controlled, thinking of Me, let him sit seeking union with Me as the Supreme.

6.15 Thus constantly seeking union with the Self, the yogī with his mind controlled, attains peace, culminating in supreme Bliss which abides in Me.

6.16   Verily, yoga is not for him who eats too much or
        does not eat at all, nor for him who sleeps too
        much or keeps awake, O Arjuna.

6.17   *To the one who is regulated in eating and
        recreation, regulated in action, who is regulated in
        sleeping and waking, yoga becomes the destroyer
        of sorrow.*

6.18   When a perfectly controlled mind rests in the Self
        alone, freed from desire for all objects, then it is
        said to be established in yoga.

6.19   As a lamp in a windless place does not flicker —
        that simile reflects a yogī with subdued mind,
        practicing union with the Self.

6.20   When the mind, restrained by the practice of yoga
        (union), comes to rest — and when seeing the Self
        alone by the self, it is satisfied in the Self.

6.21   When he knows the supreme Bliss, which can be
        grasped by the intellect, which transcends the
        senses, and wherein established, he never moves
        from Reality.

6.22   And having obtained which, he thinks no other gain
        superior to It, wherein established, *he is not moved
        even by great sorrow.*

6.23   Let that be known as the yoga of severance from
        the union with pain. That yoga should be practiced
        with determination and with an undespairing
        mind.

6.24 Abandoning without reserve all desires born of thoughts and completely restraining the group of senses from all quarters by the mind.

6.25 Little by little, let him withdraw by the intellect held firm; having established the mind in the Self, let him not think of anything else.

6.26 By whatever cause, the unsteady and restless mind wanders away, restraining it from that, let him bring it under the control of the Self alone.

6.27 Verily, supreme Bliss comes to this yogī whose mind is perfectly tranquil, whose passion is calmed, who is sinless and has become Brahman.

6.28 Thus constantly practicing union with the Self, the yogī, freed from sin (agitation), easily attains the infinite bliss of contact with Brahman.

6.29 United to the Self by yoga, he sees the Self in all beings and all beings in the Self; he sees the same everywhere.

6.30 He who sees Me everywhere and sees all in Me, I am not lost to him, nor is he lost to Me.

6.31 He who, established in oneness, worships Me abiding in all beings, that yogī dwells in Me, whatever be his mode of living.

6.32 He who, through the likeness of the Self, O Arjuna, sees equality everywhere through joy and sorrow, he is considered a supreme yogī.

6.33 Arjuna said: This yoga of equanimity taught by you, O Krishna, I do not see its enduring stability, owing to restlessness.

6.34 The mind verily, O Krishna, is restless, turbulent, strong and obstinate; I consider it as difficult to control as the wind.

6.35 The blessed Lord said: Doubtless, the mind is restless and difficult to control, O Arjuna, but it can be controlled by practice and dispassion.

6.36 Yoga, I think is hard to attain by one who is uncontrolled, but it can be attained by one who is controlled by means of striving.

6.37 Arjuna said: The uncontrolled who possesses śraddhā (determined faith), whose mind wanders away from yoga, failing to attain perfection in yoga, what end, O Krishna, does he meet?

6.38 Fallen from both, does he not perish like a rent cloud (small, separated cloud), O Krishna, supportless and deluded in the path of Brahman?

6.39 This doubt of mine, O Krishna, you should dispel completely, for there is none other than you to dispel this doubt.

6.40 The blessed Lord said: O Arjuna, neither here nor even hereafter is there destruction for him; verily none who does good, O beloved, comes to grief.

6.41 Having attained to the worlds of the righteous and having dwelt there for eternal years, he who has fallen from yoga is born in the home of the pure and wealthy.

6.42   Or he is born into a family of wise yogīs only, verily, a birth such as this is very difficult to obtain in this world.

6.43   There, united with the knowledge acquired in his former body, he strives more than before for perfection, O Arjuna.

6.44   By that former practice alone, he is borne irresistibly. Even wishing to know yoga, he goes beyond word-Brahman (talking about Brahman).

6.45   But the yogī striving with consistent attention, completely purified of sins, perfected through many births, then reaches the supreme Goal.

6.46   The yogī is deemed superior to the ascetics, superior to even the wise and superior to performers of action; therefore be a yogī O Arjuna.

6.47   And of all yogīs, he who, with the inner self absorbed in Me, worships Me with śraddhā (determined faith), he is considered by Me to be wholly united.

7.

THE YOGA OF KNOWLEDGE AND WISDOM

7.1   The blessed Lord said: O Arjuna, with the mind
        attached to Me, practicing yoga, taking refuge in
        Me, how you shall without doubt, know Me fully,
        that you do hear.

7.2   I will declare to you in full this knowledge, together
        with wisdom, which having known, nothing more
        here remains to be known.

7.3   Among thousands of men, scarce one strives for
        perfection; of those who strive and succeed, scarce
        one knows Me in essence.

7.4   Earth, water, fire, air, space, mind, intellect, and
        also ego — such is the eightfold division of My
        prakṛti (nature).

7.5   This is the lower. But different from it, O Arjuna,
        know My higher prakṛti (nature), the life-element
        by which this universe is supported.

7.6   Know this to be the womb of all beings. I am the
        origin and dissolution of the whole universe.

7.7   There is naught higher than Me, O Arjuna; all this is
        strung on Me as rows of gems on a string.

7.8   O Arjuna, I am the sapidity in waters, radiance in
        sun and moon, praṇava (syllable Om) in all the
        Vedas, sound in space, manhood in all men.

7.9   I am the sweet fragrance in earth and the brilliance
        in fire, I am the life in all beings and the austerity in
        ascetics.

7.10   O Arjuna, know Me as the eternal seed of all
        beings. I am the intelligence of the intelligent, the
        splendor of the splendid.

7.11   I am the strength of the strong devoid of desire
        and attachment, in beings, I am desire which is not
        contrary to dharma (order of the Vedas), O Arjuna.

7.12   And whatever natures that are sāttvika, rājasika
        and tāmasika — these know as from Me alone; I
        am not in them, but they are in Me.

7.13   Deluded by these natures composed of the three
        guṇas (qualities), all this world does not know Me
        well, as above them and immutable.

7.14   Verily, this divine illusion of Mine, made of guṇas
        (qualities) is difficult to cross over; those who seek
        Me alone cross over this illusion.

7.15   The evildoers, the deluded, the lowest of men do
        not seek Me, they whose wisdom is destroyed by
        illusion follow the way of the demons.

7.16   O Arjuna, four kinds of virtuous people worship
        Me — the ārtaḥ (distressed), the jijñāsuḥ (seeker
        of knowledge), the arthārthī (seeker of wealth) and
        the jñānī (wise), O Arjuna.

7.17   Of them, the jñānī (the wise), ever steadfast with
        single-pointed devotion excels; for, I am extremely
        dear to the jñānī (the wise) and they are dear to
        Me.

7.18 Noble indeed are all these, but the jñānī (the wise) I deem as verily Myself; for, steadfast in mind, he is established in Me alone as the supreme Goal.

7.19 At the end of many births, the person of wisdom reaches Me realizing that all is Vāsudeva (Reality). Such a great soul is very difficult to find.

7.20 Those deprived of wisdom approach other gods through various desires, resorting to corresponding rites led by their own nature.

7.21 *Whatever form a devotee seeks to worship with śraddhā (determined faith) I make that śraddhā of his unswerving.*

7.22 Endowed with that śraddhā (determined faith), he seeks the worship of that (form), and from it he fulfills his desires, these being verily ordained by Me alone.

7.23 Finite indeed is the fruit (accruing) to those who are of small intelligence. The worshippers of the gods go to the gods, likewise My devotees reach Me.

7.24 The foolish think of Me, the Unmanifest, as having manifestation, not knowing My supreme nature, immutable, unsurpassed.

7.25 Veiled by Yogamāyā (illusion born of the union of the three guṇas — qualities), I am not manifest to all. This deluded world knows Me not, the Unborn, the Imperishable.

7.26   O Arjuna, I know the beings of the past, present, and future, but no one knows Me.

7.27   O Arjuna, by the delusion of the pairs of opposites arising from desire and aversion, all beings are subject to illusion at birth.

7.28   But those of virtuous deeds whose sins have come to an end, they, freed from the delusion of pairs of opposites, worship Me with firm resolve.

7.29   Those who strive for liberation from old age and death, taking refuge in Me, they realize the whole — Brahman, Adhyātma (individual Self), and all karma (action).

7.30   Those who know Me with adhibhūta (above elements), adhidaiva (above gods) and adhiyajña (above sacrifice), even at the time of death, they, steadfast in mind, know Me.

8.

THE YOGA OF IMPERISHABLE BRAHMAN

8.1   Arjuna said: What is that Brahman, what is Adhyātma (Inner Self), what is karma (action) O Krishna? What is called Adhibhūta (above elements), and what is termed as Adhidaiva (above gods)?

8.2   Who and how is Adhiyajñah (above sacrifice) here in this body O Krishna? And how are you to be known at the time of death by the self-controlled?

8.3   The blessed Lord said: Brahman is the Imperishable, the Supreme. His own being is called Adhyātma (Inner Self). The creative force that causes the birth of beings is called karma (action).

8.4   Adhibhūtam is the perishable nature and Adhidaivatam is the indweller. I alone am the Adhiyajñah here in the body, O best of the embodied.

8.5   And he who casting off the body, goes forth thinking of Me alone at the time of death, he attains My Being; there is no doubt about this.

8.6   Of whatever being one thinks at the end while leaving the body, to that alone one goes, O Arjuna, (because) of constantly thinking of that being.

8.7   Therefore, at all times, remember Me and fight. With mind and intellect absorbed in Me, you shall without doubt come to Me alone.

8.8   With the unswerving mind made steadfast by the practice of yoga and meditating, O Arjuna, one goes to the supreme, resplendent Being.

8.9   He who meditates on the Omniscient, Ancient, All-ruler, minuter than the minute, supporter of all, of inconceivable form, effulgent as the sun, beyond darkness.

8.10   At the time of death, with steady mind and devotion, united by the power of yoga, and only by fixing the prāṇa (life-breath) perfectly in the middle of the two eyebrows, he reaches the supreme, resplendent Being.

8.11   That which the knowers of the Veda call the Imperishable, that which ascetics freed from passion enter, that desiring which they practice brahmacharya (non-attachment), that goal I will declare to you in brief.

8.12   Having controlled all gates, having confined the mind in the heart, having fixed his prāṇa (life-breath) in the head, established in yogic concentration.

8.13   Reciting Brahman, the one-syllabled Om, remembering Me, he who departs, leaving the body, attains the supreme Goal.

8.14   I am easily attainable by that ever steadfast yogī whose mind constantly and continuously thinks of Me without any other thought, O Arjuna.

8.15   Having come to Me, the Mahātmās (great souls)
       are no more subject to rebirth which is transitory
       and the abode of pain; they have reached the
       highest Perfection.

8.16   All the worlds up to Brahmaloka (world of Brahmā)
       are subject to return, O Arjuna, but on reaching
       Me, there is no rebirth, O Arjuna.

8.17   The people who know the day of Brahmā which
       ends in a thousand yugas (ages) and the night
       which ends in a thousand yugas, they know day
       and night.

8.18   At the approach of day all the manifested stream
       forth from the unmanifested; at the approach of
       night, they dissolve there only, in what is called the
       unmanifested.

8.19   This multitude of beings, being born again and
       again, is dissolved helplessly at the approach
       of night, O Arjuna, and it streams forth at the
       approach of day.

8.20   But there exists higher than the unmanifested, yet
       another unmanifested Being, eternal, which is not
       destroyed when all beings are destroyed.

8.21   The Unmanifested is called the Imperishable. It is
       said to be the ultimate goal. Those who reach It do
       not return. That is My supreme Abode.

8.22 O Arjuna, that supreme Being in whom all beings dwell, by whom all this is pervaded is indeed attainable by unswerving devotion.

8.23 I will tell you indeed, O Arjuna, the time in which yogīs departing never return and also the time they do return.

8.24 Fire, light, day-time, the bright-fortnight, the six months of the northern path (of the Sun) — there departing, the knowers of Brahman go to Brahman.

8.25 Smoke, night-time, dark-fortnight, the six months of the southern path (of the Sun) — there obtaining the lunar light, the yogī returns.

8.26 These bright and dark paths of the world are verily deemed eternal; by the one (a person) goes not to return, by the other, they return again.

8.27 Knowing these two paths, O Arjuna, no yogī is deluded; therefore, O Arjuna, be steadfast in yoga at all times.

8.28 Whatever meritorious fruit is assigned to Vedas, sacrifices, austerities, and also to gifts — the yogī rises above all these by having known this and goes to the supreme, primeval Abode.

9.

THE YOGA OF ROYAL KNOWLEDGE AND ROYAL SECRET

9.1 The blessed Lord said: To you who does not make
unnecessary objections, verily, I shall declare
the greatest secret — knowledge together with
wisdom — which, having known, you shall be free
from evil.

9.2 The royal knowledge, the royal secret, the supreme
purifier is this, directly realizable, righteous, very
easy to practice, imperishable.

9.3 O Arjuna, those devoid of śraddhā (determined
faith) in this dharma (supreme Knowledge),
without attaining Me, return to the path of the
mortal world.

9.4 All this world is pervaded by Me in the
unmanifested form; all beings dwell in Me, and I do
not dwell in them.

9.5 Nor do beings dwell in Me; behold My divine yoga!
Bringing forth and supporting beings, My Self does
not dwell in them.

9.6 As the mighty wind moving everywhere rests ever
in space, even so, know that all beings rest in Me.

9.7 O Arjuna, at the end of a kalpa (time-cycle) all
beings enter My prakṛti (nature); at the beginning
of a kalpa I bring them forth again.

9.8 Animating My own prakṛti (nature) I bring forth
again and again all this multitude of beings,
helpless by the force of prakṛti.

9.9   Nor do these acts, O Arjuna, bind Me, remaining like one unconcerned and unattached to those acts.

9.10   By Me presiding, prakṛti (nature) produces the moving and the unmoving; because of this, O Arjuna, the world revolves.

9.11   Fools disregard Me dwelling in the human form, not knowing My supreme nature, the great Lord of beings.

9.12   Of vain hopes, of vain actions, of vain knowledge, senseless, they verily are possessed of the delusive prakṛti (nature) of rākṣasas and asuras.

9.13   But Mahātmās (great souls), O Arjuna, possessed of My divine nature, worship Me with unwavering mind, having known Me to be the imperishable Source of beings.

9.14   Always glorifying Me, striving, firm in vows, prostrating before Me with devotion, ever steadfast, they worship Me.

9.15   Yet others sacrificing by the yajña (sacrifice) of knowledge worship Me as one, as distinct and as manifold facing all directions.

9.16   I am kratu (Vedic ritual), I am yajña (sacrifice), I am svadhā (ancestral offering), I am auṣadha (medicinal herb), I am mantra (chant), I am ājya (clarified butter), I am agni (fire), I am huta (burnt offering).

9.17   I am the father of this world, mother, sustainer,
        grandfather, that which is to be known, purifier, the
        syllable Om, and also Ṛk, Sāma and Yajuḥ.

9.18   The goal, supporter, Lord, witness, abode, shelter,
        friend, origin, dissolution, substratum, treasure-
        house, the imperishable seed.

9.19   I give heat, I withhold and send forth rain; I am
        immortality as well as death, being and non-being,
        O Arjuna.

9.20   The knowers of the three Vedas, drinkers of soma
        (herbal juice), purified of pāpas (sins), worshipping
        Me by yajñas (sacrifices), pray for passage to
        heaven, they, reaching the holy world of the lord of
        the gods enjoy the divine pleasures of the gods in
        heaven.

9.21   They, having enjoyed that vast world of heaven,
        their puṇya (merit) exhausted, enter the world
        of mortals; thus abiding by the injunctions of the
        three (Vedas), desiring objects of desires, they
        attain the state of going and coming.

9.22   To those persons who worship Me, thinking of
        nothing else, to those ever seeking union I grant
        them yoga (union) and kṣema (supreme bliss).

9.23   Even those devotees who, endowed with śraddhā
        (determined faith) worship other gods, they also
        worship Me alone, O Arjuna, though contrary to
        traditional practice.

9.24   I am indeed the Enjoyer and also the Lord of all
        yajñas (sacrifices), but they do not know Me in
        reality; hence they fall.

9.25   Those who worship the devas (senses) go to devas,
        the worshippers of ancestors go to ancestors, the
        worshippers of the elements go to elements, and
        those who worship Me come to Me.

9.26   Whosoever with devotion offers Me a leaf, a
        flower, a fruit, water; that devout offering of the
        striving self I accept.

9.27   Whatever you do, whatever you eat, whatever you
        offer, whatever you give, whatever austerity you
        practice, O Arjuna, do that as an offering to Me.

9.28   Thus you shall be freed from the bonds of actions
        bearing good and evil results; seeking union by
        sannyāsayoga (yoga of renunciation), liberated, you
        shall come to Me.

9.29   The same am I in all beings, there is none hateful
        or dear to Me; but those who worship Me with
        devotion, they are in Me, and I am also in them.

9.30   Even if a very wicked person worships Me with
        unswerving devotion, he too shall be regarded as
        righteous indeed for he has rightly resolved.

9.31   Soon he becomes righteous and attains eternal
        peace, O Arjuna, know for certain that My devotee
        never perishes.

9.32 For those who take refuge in Me, O Arjuna, though
      of agitated birth — whatever their birth, race, or
      gender — they also attain the supreme Goal.

9.33 So much more than holy brahmins and devout
      royal-sages! Having reached this transient joyless
      world, you worship Me.

9.34 Fix your mind on Me, be devoted to Me, sacrifice
      to Me, bow down to Me; thus uniting yourself
      to Me, taking Me as the supreme Goal, you will
      certainly come to Me.

10.

THE YOGA OF SUPREME MANIFESTATION

10.1 The blessed Lord said: O Arjuna, listen again to My supreme word, which I will speak to you who are delighted, for your welfare.

10.2 Neither the hosts of gods nor the great sages know My origin, for in all respects, I am the source of all the gods and the great sages.

10.3 He who knows Me as unborn, beginningless, and the supreme Lord of the world, he, undeluded among mortals, is liberated of all sins (agitations).

10.4 Intellect, knowledge, non-illusion, forgiveness, truth, control over senses and mind, joy and sorrow, existence and non-existence, fear and fearlessness, also

10.5 Non-injury, equanimity, contentment, austerity, charity, fame and infamy — different kinds of characteristics of beings arise from Me alone.

10.6 The seven great sages, the ancient four and the Manus, with their being in Me, were born of mind; from them are these creatures of the world.

10.7 He who knows in reality this supreme manifestation and My yoga (union), he becomes established in unshakable union; there is no doubt about it.

10.8 I am the origin of all, from Me everything evolves; understanding thus, the wise worship Me, endowed with devotion.

10.9   Those with mind in Me, with prāṇas (life's activities) absorbed in Me, enlightening one another and always speaking of Me, they are contented and delighted.

10.10   To those, ever steadfast, worshiping Me with love (identification), I give the buddhi-yoga (union by intellect) by which they come to Me.

10.11   Out of mere compassion for them dwelling as Self, I dispel the darkness born of ignorance by the shining lamp of wisdom.

10.12   Arjuna said: You are the supreme Brahman, the supreme Abode, the supreme Purifier, the eternal, divine Puruṣa (Being), the primeval God, unborn, all-pervading.

10.13   All the sages acclaim Thee, also the divine sage Nārada, Asita, Devala, Vyāsa, and so do You, Yourself, say to me.

10.14   I regard all this that You say to me as true, O Krishna. Verily, O blessed Lord, neither the gods nor the demons know Your manifestation.

10.15   Verily, You Yourself know Yourself by Yourself, O Krishna, O Source of beings, O Lord of beings, O God of gods, O Ruler of the world.

10.16   You should indeed speak without reserve of Your divine glories, by which glories pervading these worlds, You exist.

10.17 How may I know You, O Krishna, through constant meditation? In what all aspects are You to be thought of by me, O blessed Lord?

10.18 Tell me again in detail, O Krishna, of Your yoga and manifestation; for there is no satiety for me in hearing the nectarine.

10.19 The blessed Lord said: Well, I will declare to you My divine glories in chief, O best of the Kurus, Arjuna, there is no end to My detailing.

10.20 I am the Self, O Arjuna, seated in the heart of all beings; I am the beginning, the middle, and also the end of all beings.

10.21 Of Ādityas I am Viṣṇu, of luminaries the radiant sun, I am Marīci of Maruts, of asterisms I am the moon.

10.22 Of Vedas I am Sāma Veda, of gods I am Vāsava, of senses I am the mind and of living beings I am Consciousness.

10.23 And of Rudras I am Śaṅkara, Vitteśa of Yakṣas and Rākṣasas, of Vasus I am Pāvaka and of mountains I am Meru.

10.24 And of household priests, O Arjuna, know me to be the chief, Bṛhaspati, of generals I am Skanda, of lakes I am the ocean.

10.25 Of the great sages I am Bhṛgu, of speech I am the one syllable (Om), of yajñas (sacrifices) I am japayajña (sacrifice of chant of the holy name), of immovables, Himālaya.

10.26 Aśvattha (Pipal tree) of all trees and of celestial sages Nārada, of Gandharvas Citraratha, of Siddhas (perfected souls) sage Kapila.

10.27 Of horses know Me as Uccaiḥśravas, born of nectar, of lordly elephants Airāvata, and of men, the king.

10.28 Of weapons I am Vajra (thunderbolt), of cows I am Kāmadhuk, and I am Kandarpa the progenitor, of serpents I am Vāsuki.

10.29 And I am Ananta of Nāgas (snakes), I am Varuṇa of water-beings, and of forefathers I am Aryamā, I am Yama of controllers.

10.30 I am Prahlāda of Daityas, I am time of reckoners, and of beasts I am the lion and Vainateya of birds.

10.31 I am the wind of purifiers, I am Rāma of warriors, and of fishes, I am the shark, of rivers, I am the Jāhnavī (Gaṅgā).

10.32 Of creations, I am the beginning and the end and also the middle, O Arjuna, of knowledges, I am the Knowledge-of-Self, of arguments, vādaḥ (logic).

10.33 Of letters, I am अ (A) and dvandvaḥ (dual) of all compounds, I am verily the everlasting time, I am the supporter facing all directions.

10.34 And I am the all-devouring death and the birth of future beings, of the feminine (I am) Kīrtiḥ (fame), Śrīḥ (prosperity), Vāk (speech), Smṛitiḥ (memory),

Medhā (intelligence), Dhṛtiḥ (firmness) and Kṣamā (forgiveness).

10.35 Also Bṛhatsāma of Sāma hymns, I am Gāyatrī of metres, of months, I am Mārgaśīrṣaḥ, of seasons, the flowery season (spring).

10.36 I am gambling of the fraudulent, I am splendour of the splendid, I am victory, I am determination, I am sattva (purity) of the sāttvika (pure).

10.37 Of the Vṛṣṇīs, I am Vāsudeva, of the Pāṇḍavas Dhanañjaya, also of sages, I am Vyāsa, of seers, the seer Uśanā.

10.38 I am the sceptre of rulers, I am righteousness of those who seek victory, and also I am silence of secrets, I am knowledge of knowers.

10.39 And also, I am that which is the seed of all beings, O Arjuna, there is no being moving or unmoving which can exist without Me.

10.40 There is no end to My divine manifestations, O Arjuna; this is only a brief statement by Me of the extent of My manifestation.

10.41 Whatever being is glorious, prosperous or powerful, know that only to be a manifestation of a part of My splendor.

10.42 But what is the knowledge of these details to you, O Arjuna? Having pervaded this entire universe by one fragment, I remain.

11.

THE YOGA OF VISION OF THE COSMIC FORM

11.1   Arjuna said: By that speech of the supreme secret known as Adhyātma (Self), which You have spoken out of compassion for me, this delusion of mine is dispelled.

11.2   Verily, the origin and dissolution of beings verily has been heard by me in detail from You, O Lotus-eyed; and also (Your) inexhaustible greatness.

11.3   O Krishna, it is just as You have declared Yourself; I desire to see Your supreme form, O Krishna.

11.4   O Lord, if you think it possible for me to see Your imperishable Self, then show me thus, O Krishna.

11.5   The blessed Lord said: Behold, O Arjuna, in hundreds and thousands, My divine forms of different kinds and of various colors and shapes.

11.6   Behold Ādityas, Vasus, Rudras, (two) Aśvins, also Maruts; behold, O Arjuna, many wonders never seen before.

11.7   Now behold here in My body, O Guḍākeśa, the whole world with the moving and the unmoving centred in one and whatever else you desire to see.

11.8   But you cannot see Me with these eyes of yours; I give you the divine eye, behold My supreme yoga.

11.9   Sañjaya said: O king, having spoken thus, the great Lord of yoga, Hari, showed His supreme divine form to Arjuna.

11.10 With many mouths and eyes, with many marvellous visions, with many divine ornaments, with many uplifted divine weapons.

11.11 Wearing divine garlands and apparel, anointed with divine scents and unguents, full of all wonders, resplendent, endless, with face on all sides.

11.12 If a thousand suns were to arise all together in the sky that splendour would be the splendour of that exalted Being.

11.13 There, in the body of the God of gods, Arjuna then saw the whole world with its manifold divisions resting in one.

11.14 Then he, Arjuna, struck with wonder, hair standing on end at the back of the neck, bowing his head to the God, spoke with joined palms.

11.15 Arjuna said: O God, I see in Your body all the gods and hosts of various beings, Brahmā, the Lord based on the lotus-seat and all sages and divine serpents.

11.16 I see You in endless form everywhere with manifold arms, stomachs, mouths and eyes; neither Your end nor middle nor also Your beginning do I see O Lord of the universe, O universal Form.

11.17 I see You with crown, mace and discus, a mass of radiance shining everywhere, hard to look at, shining all around like the glorious fire and sun, immeasurable.

11.18 I consider you to be the Imperishable, Supreme to be known, You to be the ultimate Abode of this universe, You to be the immutable Protector of eternal dharma (laws); You to be the ancient Puruṣa (Being).

11.19 I see You without beginning, middle or end, infinite in power, with endless arms, the sun and moon as (Your) eyes, shining fire as mouth, heating this universe with Your radiance.

11.20 Heaven and earth, this interspace and all the quarters are indeed pervaded by You alone; having seen this marvellous and awful form of Yours the triple world trembles, O Great Soul.

11.21 Verily, into You enter these hosts of gods, some in fright, extol you with joined palms, May it be well, thus saying, bands of great sages and siddhas (perfected ones) praise you with beautiful hymns.

11.22 The Rudras, Ādityas, Vasus, Sādhyas, Viśvedevas, Aśvins, Maruts, Ūṣmapas and hosts of Gandharvas, Yakṣas, Asuras and Siddhas — all these behold You quite astonished.

11.23 Seeing your mighty form with many mouths and eyes, many arms, thighs and feet, many stomachs, many terrible tusks, O Krishna, the worlds are terrified, so am I.

11.24 Seeing You touching the sky, shining in many colours, with mouths open, with large shining eyes, my mind is terrified and I find no courage or peace, O Krishna.

11.25 Seeing Your mouths with terrible tusks and blazing like fires of time, I know not the (four) quarters and find no peace; have mercy O Lord of gods, O Abode of the universe.

11.26 These sons of Dhṛtarāṣṭra with all the hosts of kings, Bhīsma, Droṇa and Sūta's son, along with our warrior-chiefs.

11.27 Into Your mouths with terrible tusks, fearful to behold, they hurriedly enter. Some are seen sticking in the gaps between the teeth with their heads pulverized.

11.28 As the many torrents of rivers rush towards the ocean alone, so do these heroes in the world of men enter Your blazing mouths.

11.29 As moths with great speed enter into the brilliant fire for destruction, even so people enter with great speed into Your mouths for destruction.

11.30 Swallowing all the people on every side with flaming mouths, You are licking. Your fierce rays, filling the whole world with radiance, are burning O Krishna.

11.31 Make known to me who You are, fierce in form. Salutation to You O Supreme God, have mercy.

I desire to know You, the Primeval, I know not indeed Your purpose.

11.32 The blessed Lord said: I am the mighty, world-destroying time engaged here in annihilating the worlds. Even without you, all these warriors arrayed in the opposing armies shall not live.

11.33 Therefore, you arise and acquire fame. Having conquered the foes, enjoy the prosperous kingdom. Verily, they have already been slain by Me, you be a mere instrument, O Arjuna.

11.34 Droṇa and Bhīṣma and Jayadratha and Karṇa as also other heroic warriors already slain by Me, you kill. Be not distressed; fight, you shall conquer the enemies in battle.

11.35 Sañjaya said: Having heard that speech of Krishna, the crowned one, Arjuna, trembling, saluting with joined palms, bowing, overwhelmed with fear spoke again to Krishna in a choked voice.

11.36 Arjuna said: Krishna, rightly the world is delighted and rejoices in Your praise; rākṣasas (demons) flee in terror in all directions and all the hosts of siddhas (perfected ones) bow.

11.37 And why not they bow to you, O exalted Self, greatest, the primal cause even of Brahmā, O Infinite Being, O Lord of gods, O Abode of the universe? You are the imperishable, the being and non-being, that which is supreme.

11.38 You are the primal God, the ancient Puruṣa (Being), supreme Abode of this universe, You are the Knower, That to be known, and the supreme Goal. By You is the universe pervaded, O Being of infinite forms.

11.39 You are Vāyu (wind god), Yama (god of death), Agni (fire god), Varuṇa (sea god), Śaśāṅka (moon), Prajāpati (Brahmā, creator) and great-grandfather; salutation, salutation to You a thousand times and again and again salutation, salutation to You!

11.40 Salutation to You before and behind, indeed salutation to You on all sides, O All! Infinite in power, infinite in strength, You complete all, wherefore You are all.

11.41 Having regarded You as a friend, whatever was rashly said by me addressing You as, 'O Krishna, O Yādava, O friend', not knowing Your greatness and out of negligence or even love...

11.42 In whatever way You have been insulted O Krishna in jest, playing, repose, seated or at meals, when alone or in company, I implore You, Immeasurable, to forgive.

11.43 You are the father of this world, of the moving and unmoving, and You are to be worshipped, greater than the great; there is none equal to You; how then would anyone excel You in the three worlds, O Being of incomparable power.

11.44   Therefore bowing down, prostrating my body
         before You, O adorable Lord, I seek Your grace. You
         should bear with me, O God, as father with son, as
         friend with friend, as lover with beloved.

11.45   Having seen what was not seen before I am
         delighted, yet my mind is distressed with fear.
         Show me, O God, that form only, have mercy O
         God of gods, O Abode of the universe.

11.46   I wish to see You as before, crowned, bearing a
         mace, with discus in hand, in that same four-armed
         form, O Thousand-armed, O Universal Form.

11.47   The blessed Lord said: By My grace O Arjuna, this
         form of Mine has been shown to you by My own
         yoga — supreme, resplendent, primeval, infinite,
         universal form of Mine which has not been seen
         before by anyone else than you.

11.48   Neither by the study of the Vedas, nor by yajñas
         (sacrifices), nor by gifts, nor by rituals, nor by
         severe austerities can I be seen in such a form in
         the world of men by anyone other than you, O
         Arjuna.

11.49   Having seen such a terrible form of Mine as this, be
         not bewildered; fearless, with a gladdened heart,
         you again behold this former form of Mine indeed.

11.50   Sañjaya said: So Krishna, having thus spoken to
         Arjuna, again revealed His own form and the Great-

soul, assuming His gentle form, pacified him who was terrified.

11.51 Arjuna said: Having seen this gentle human form of Yours, O Krishna, with mind composed, I am now restored to my nature.

11.52 The blessed Lord said: Very hard to see is this form of Mine which you have seen; even the gods ever long to behold this form...

11.53 Neither by Vedas, nor by penance, or gift, nor by sacrifice can I be seen like this as you have seen Me.

11.54 But by single-pointed devotion, I may be seen like this, O Arjuna and known in reality and entered, O Arjuna.

11.55 He who performs actions for Me, with Me as Supreme is devoted to Me, free from attachment, without enmity towards any being — he reaches Me, O Arjuna.

12.

THE YOGA OF DEVOTION

12.1   Arjuna said: Thus, those ever steadfast devotees who worship You and also those who worship the Imperishable, the Unmanifest, which of these are best versed in yoga?

12.2   The blessed Lord said: Those ever steadfast (devotees) who, fixing mind on Me, worship Me endowed with supreme śraddhā (determined faith), them do I consider best in yoga.

12.3   Those, indeed, who worship the Imperishable, Indefinable, Unmanifest, Omnipresent, Unthinkable, Unchanging, Immovable and Eternal.

12.4   Having well restrained the group of senses, regarding everything equally, rejoicing in the welfare of all beings, they also reach Me.

12.5   Greater is their difficulty whose minds are set on the Unmanifest, for the goal, the Unmanifest, is hard for the embodied to reach.

12.6   But those who worship Me, renouncing all actions in Me, regarding Me as supreme, meditating on Me with single-pointed yoga...

12.7   For those whose minds are set on Me, I become near, O Arjuna, the deliverer from the ocean of death-bound saṁsāra (mundane, cycle of birth-death existence).

12.8   *Fix your mind on Me alone, place your intellect in Me; you shall then no doubt live in Me alone henceforth.*

12.9   *If you are unable to fix your mind steadily on Me,
then seek to reach Me by abhyāsa yoga (yoga of
practice), O Arjuna.*

12.10   *If you are incapable of even abhyāsa (practice)
regard My action as supreme; even by performing
actions for My sake you shall attain Perfection.*

12.11   *If you are unable to do even this, then taking
refuge in the union with Me, renounce the fruits of
all actions, self-controlled.*

12.12   *Better indeed is knowledge than practice; better
than knowledge is meditation; (better) than
meditation is renunciation of the fruit of action;
peace immediately follows renunciation.*

12.13   *Not hating any being, friendly and compassionate,
free from attachment and egoism, balanced in
pleasure and pain and forgiving.*

12.14   *Ever-perfectly content, yogī (uniting with Self), self-
controlled, having firm conviction, with mind and
intellect dedicated to Me, My devotee is dear to
Me.*

12.15   *By whom the world is not agitated and who is not
agitated by the world, who is freed from joy, envy,
fear and anxiety — they are dear to Me.*

12.16   *Free from wants, pure, dexterous, unconcerned,
untroubled, renouncer of all undertakings — My
devotee is dear to Me.*

12.17   *The one who neither rejoices nor hates, nor grieves,
        nor desires, renouncer of good and evil, who is full
        of devotion, is dear to Me.*

12.18   *Alike to friend and foe and also to honour and
        dishonour, alike to heat and cold, to joy and sorrow,
        entirely free from attachment.*

12.19   *To whom censure and praise are equal, silent,
        content with anything, homeless, steady-minded,
        the person full of devotion is dear to Me.*

12.20   *They, indeed, who follow this immortal dharma
        (law) as declared, endued with śraddhā
        (determined faith), regarding Me as supreme —
        those devotees are exceedingly dear to Me.*

13.

THE YOGA OF THE DISTINCTION BETWEEN FIELD AND KNOWER OF FIELD

13.1   Arjuna said: Prakṛti (matter) and Puruṣa (Spirit), also kṣetra (field) and Kṣetrajña (Knower of field) and also Knowledge and That which ought to be known — these I wish to learn O Krishna.

13.2   The blessed Lord said: This body, O Arjuna, is called kṣetra (field); he who knows this is called Kṣetrajña (Knower of field) by those who know of That.

13.3   And O Arjuna, also know Me as the Kṣetrajña Knower in all kṣetras fields; the knowledge of kṣetra and Kṣetrajña that is considered by Me to be Knowledge.

13.4   What that kṣetra field is and what it is like, what are its modifications and whence it is and also what He is and what His power is — that, hear from Me in brief.

13.5   Sung by sages in many ways, in various hymns as also in distinctive precepts indicating Brahman, full of reason and certainty.

13.6   The great elements, ego, intellect and also the unmanifest, the ten senses and the one (mind) and the five objects of the senses.

13.7   Desire, hatred, pleasure, pain, assemblage (body), intelligence, firmness; this is kṣetra (field) briefly described with its modifications.

13.8   Humility, unpretentiousness, harmlessness, forgiveness, uprightness, service of the preceptor, purity, steadfastness, self-control.

13.9   Dispassion towards sense objects and also absence of egoism, perception of pain and evil of birth, disease, old age and death.

13.10   Non-attachment, non-infatuation with child, wife or home and constant balance of mind in desirable and undesirable happenings.

13.11   Unswerving devotion to Me by steadfast yoga, resorting to solitary place and distaste for crowd of people.

13.12   Constancy in Self-knowledge, perception of end of true knowledge. This is declared to be knowledge, what is opposed to this is ignorance.

13.13   I will declare That which has to be known, which having known one enjoys immortality; beginningless is the supreme Brahman. That is called neither sat (existent) nor asat (non-existent).

13.14   With hands and feet everywhere, with eyes, heads and mouths everywhere, with ears everywhere That exists in the world enveloping all.

13.15   Shining by the functions of all the senses without any senses, unattached yet supporting all, devoid of gunas qualities and enjoying the gunas.

13.16   Without and within beings, the unmoving and also the moving; That is incomprehensible due to subtlety and That is far and near.

13.17 Undivided and yet existing as if divided in beings
and That which is to be known is the sustainer of
beings, destroyer and creator.

13.18 The Light even of lights, That is said to be beyond
darkness; Knowledge, That which is to be known,
Goal of knowledge, seated in the hearts of all.

13.19 Thus the kṣetra field as well as Knowledge and That
which has to be known have been briefly stated;
knowing this, My devotee attains My being.

13.20 Know that prakṛti (matter) and Puruṣa (Spirit)
are both beginningless and know also that
modifications and guṇas qualities are born of
prakṛti.

13.21 In the production of effect and cause, prakṛti
matter is said to be the cause; in the experience
of pleasure and pain Puruṣa Spirit is said to be the
cause.

13.22 Puruṣa Spirit seated in prakṛti matter indeed
experiences the guṇas qualities born of prakṛti;
attachment to the guṇas is the cause of its birth in
good and evil wombs.

13.23 The supreme Puruṣa Spirit in this body is thus said
to be the witness, permitter, supporter, enjoyer,
great lord and also the supreme Self.

13.24 He who knows Puruṣa (Spirit) and prakṛti (matter)
together with the guṇas (qualities), though living in
whatever way, he is not born again.

13.25　Some by meditation behold the Self in the self by the self, others by Sāṅkhya yoga, yoga of knowledge, and others by Karma yoga, yoga of action.

13.26　Yet others, not knowing thus, worship the Supreme having heard from others, and they too cross beyond death taking refuge in what they have heard.

13.27　Whatever being is born, moving or unmoving, O Arjuna, know that to be the union of kṣetra field and Kṣetrajña Knower of field.

13.28　He who sees the supreme Lord abiding equally in all beings as the Imperishable among the perishable — he sees.

13.29　Seeing indeed the same Lord dwelling equally everywhere he does not destroy the Self by the self, he then reaches the supreme Goal.

13.30　He who sees all action as performed by prakṛti (matter) alone and also the Self as actionless, he sees.

13.31　When he perceives the diversified existence of beings as rooted in One and spreading forth from That alone then he becomes Brahman.

13.32　Being without beginning or guṇas (qualities), this supreme Self, imperishable, though dwelling in the body, O Arjuna, neither acts nor is tainted.

13.33 As the all-pervading space is not tainted due
to its subtlety, so the Self, seated in the body
everywhere, is not tainted.

13.34 As the one sun illumines this whole world, so does
the Kṣetrī Lord-of-field illumine the whole kṣetra
field, O Arjuna.

13.35 They who with the Eye of Wisdom perceive thus,
the distinction between kṣetra field and Kṣetrajña
Knower of field and the liberation of beings from
prakṛti (matter), they go to the Supreme.

14.

THE YOGA OF DISTINCTION OF THE THREE GUNAS

14.1 The blessed Lord said: I will again declare the supreme Knowledge, the best of knowledges, which having known all sages have gone from here to ultimate perfection.

14.2 Having taken refuge in this knowledge and attained unity with Me, they are neither born even in creation nor disturbed in dissolution.

14.3 My womb is great Brahmā, in that I place the seed; thence arises birth of all beings, O Arjuna.

14.4 Whatever forms are produced in all wombs O Arjuna, great Brahmā is their womb, I the seed-giving Father.

14.5 Sattva, rajas, tamas — these guṇas (qualities) born of prakṛti (matter) bind the indestructible Embodied to the body, O Arjuna.

14.6 Of these, sattva being stainless, is luminous and healthy; it binds through attachment to happiness and attachment to knowledge, O Arjuna.

14.7 Know rajas to be of the nature of passion, the source of thirst and attachment; it binds fast O Arjuna, the embodied by attachment to action.

14.8 But know tamas to be born of ignorance, the deluder of all embodied; it binds fast through heedlessness, indolence and sleep, O Arjuna.

14.9 Sattva attaches to happiness, rajas to action O Arjuna, while tamas indeed, having veiled knowledge, attaches to heedlessness.

14.10 Sattva arises having predominated over rajas and tamas O Arjuna, and rajas over sattva and tamas, even so, tamas over sattva and rajas.

14.11 When the light of wisdom streams forth through all the gates in this body, then it may be known that sattva indeed is predominant.

14.12 Greed, activity, undertaking of works, unrest, longing — these arise when rajas predominates, O Arjuna.

14.13 Darkness, inertness, recklessness and also delusion — these arise when tamas predominates, O Arjuna.

14.14 When the embodied being indeed meets death in the predominance of sattva, then he attains to the spotless worlds of the knowers of the Supreme.

14.15 Meeting death in rajas, he is born among those attached to action; so also, dying in tamas he is born in the wombs of the senseless.

14.16 The fruit of good action they say is sāttvika (pure), while the fruit of rajas is sorrow; the fruit of tamas, ignorance.

14.17 From sattva, arises knowledge and from rajas greed, from tamas arises recklessness and delusion and also ignorance.

14.18 Those established in sattva move upwards, the rājasika remain in the middle, the tāmasika following the course of the lowest guṇa quality, go downwards.

14.19   When the seer perceives no agent other than the guṇas (qualities) and knows the Higher beyond the guṇas, he attains My being.

14.20   Having crossed over these three guṇas (qualities), the dweller in the body is completely freed from birth, death, old age and pain arising from the body and attains immortality.

14.21   Arjuna said: What marks has he who has crossed over these three guṇas (qualities), O Lord? What is his conduct and how does he go beyond these three guṇas?

14.22   The blessed Lord said: Light, activity and even delusion O Arjuna, he hates not when present nor longs for them when absent.

14.23   He who, seated like one unconcerned, is not moved by guṇas (qualities); who, realizing that only guṇas function, is firm and moves not.

14.24   He to whom joy and sorrow are same, rooted in Self, to whom a clod of earth, stone and gold are same, to whom pleasant and unpleasant are alike, the wise, to him much censure and praise are alike.

14.25   Alike in honour and dishonour, alike to friend and foe, relinquishing all undertakings, he is said to have crossed over the guṇas (qualities).

14.26 And he who serves Me with unswerving yoga of
       devotion, he, having duly crossed these guṇas, is fit
       for becoming Brahman.

14.27 For I am the abode of Brahman, immortal,
       immutable, eternal dharma Being and absolute
       bliss.

15.

THE YOGA OF
THE SUPREME BEING

15.1   The blessed Lord said: They speak of the imperishable Aśvattha giant fig tree with root above, branches below, whose leaves are hymns of Vedas; he who knows that, gains wisdom of Vedas.

15.2   Its branches spread below and above nourished by the guṇas (qualities), with buds as sense objects and roots stretching below as actions binding men in the world.

15.3   Its form is not perceived here as such, neither its end nor origin nor clear foundation; having cut asunder this firmly-rooted Aśvattha giant fig tree with the strong axe of non-attachment...

15.4   Then that Goal should be sought, whither having gone they do not return again. I seek refuge in that primeval Puruṣa supreme Being alone wherefrom streamed forth ancient activity.

15.5   Freed from pride and delusion, evils of attachment conquered, ever-rooted in Self, desires having completely gone, well-liberated from pairs of opposites, like joy and sorrow, the undeluded reach that eternal Goal.

15.6   That the sun illumines not, nor moon, nor fire; whither having gone they return not, that is My supreme Abode.

15.7   A portion of My eternal Self having become a being in the living world, abiding in prakṛti (matter) attracts the senses with mind as the sixth.

15.8   When the Lord acquires a body and also when He leaves it, He takes these and goes as wind carries the scents from their seat.

15.9   Presiding over the ear, eye, skin, tongue, nose and also the mind, this (Being) enjoys the objects of senses.

15.10   *(This Being) departing or dwelling or enjoying united with the guṇas (qualities) the deluded do not perceive; those with the Eye of Wisdom see.*

15.11   The yogīs who strive perceive This dwelling in the self, the unrefined and unintelligent, even though striving, do not perceive This.

15.12   The light residing in the sun which illumines the whole world, which is in moon and in fire, know that light to be Mine.

15.13   Permeating the earth I support beings by energy, and having become the juicy moon, I nourish all plants.

15.14   Having become Vaiśvānara fire, abiding in the body of living beings, united with prāṇa inhalation and apāna exhalation, I digest the fourfold food.

15.15   I am seated in the hearts of all and from Me (emanate) memory, knowledge and (their) loss; I am verily That which is to be known by the Vedas, I am indeed the author of Vedānta and the knower of the Vedas.

15.16 There are these two puruṣas (beings) in the
world — the perishable and the imperishable; the
perishable is all beings and the imperishable is
called kūṭastha immutable.

15.17 But the highest Puruṣa (Being) is another, called
the supreme Self, the indestructible Lord, who
pervades and sustains the three worlds.

15.18 As I transcend the perishable and am even higher
than the Imperishable, I am therefore proclaimed
in the world and in the Veda as Puruṣottama
(Supreme Being).

15.19 The undeluded who knows Me thus as
Puruṣottama (Supreme Being) he, all-knowing,
worships Me with his whole being, O Arjuna.

15.20 Thus, this most secret science has been declared
by Me; knowing this one becomes wise and
fulfilled of duties, O Arjuna.

16.

THE YOGA OF DISTINCTION OF DIVINE AND DEMONIAC NATURE

16.1   The blessed Lord said: Fearlessness, complete purity, steadfastness in knowledge and yoga, charity, self-restraint and yajña (sacrifice), self-study, austerity and uprightness.

16.2   Harmlessness, truth, absence of anger, renunciation, peace, absence of slander, compassion for beings, uncovetousness, gentleness, modesty, absence of fickleness.

16.3   Spiritual lustre, forgiveness, steadfastness, purity, absence of malice, absence of much pride — these belong to one born of divine state, O Arjuna.

16.4   Ostentation, arrogance, self-conceit and anger, also harshness and ignorance belong, O Arjuna, to one born of demoniac nature.

16.5   The divine nature is deemed for liberation, the demoniac for bondage; grieve not, you are born of the divine nature O Arjuna.

16.6   The two created beings in this world are the divine and demoniac. The divine has been described in detail; hear from Me O Arjuna, the demoniac.

16.7   The demoniac people do not know action from inaction; also neither purity nor good conduct nor truth is found in them.

16.8   They say, The world is without Reality, without foundation, without Lord, born of mutual union caused by lust — what else?

16.9   Holding this view, the ruined souls of small
         intellect, of fierce deeds, come forth as enemies
         for the destruction of the world.

16.10   Abiding in insatiable desire, overpowered by
         hypocrisy, pride and arrogance, gripped by evil
         ideas through delusion, they work with impure
         resolve.

16.11   Beset with immense care ending only with death,
         with sensual enjoyments their highest aim, feeling
         sure 'this is all'.

16.12   Bound by hundreds of bands of hope, succumbing
         to lust and wrath, they strive to obtain hoards of
         wealth unjustly for sensual enjoyment.

16.13   "This today have I gained, this object of desire I
         shall obtain; this is mine, also this wealth shall
         continue to be mine in future."

16.14   "This enemy I have slain, and others also I shall
         slay; I am the lord, I am the enjoyer, I am perfect,
         powerful, happy."

16.15   "I am rich, well-born; who else is equal to me? I
         will sacrifice, I will give, I will rejoice" — thus are
         they deluded by ignorance.

16.16   Bewildered by many a fancy, entangled in the web
         of delusion, addicted to sensual enjoyments, they
         fall into a foul hell.

16.17   Self-conceited, stubborn, overpowered by the
         pride and arrogance of wealth, they perform

sacrifices in name, out of ostentation, contrary to ordinance (narcissism and not altruism).

16.18 Given over to egoism, power, haughtiness, lust and wrath, the malicious people detest Me in their own and in others' bodies.

16.19 These cruel haters, worst of men, I hurl these evildoers forever in the worlds only in demoniac wombs.

16.20 Having fallen into demoniac wombs the deluded, birth after birth without reaching Me, thence pass into a still lower state O Arjuna.

16.21 Triple is this gate of hell, destructive of the Self — desire, anger and greed; therefore one should abandon these three.

16.22 Liberated from these three gates of darkness O Arjuna, man does good to himself, thence reaches the supreme Goal.

16.23 He who casts aside scriptural ordinance and acts under the impulse of desire attains neither perfection, nor happiness, nor the supreme Goal.

16.24 Therefore, the scripture is your authority in determining what ought to be done and what ought not to be done; having known what is pronounced in scriptural ordinance, you should perform action here.

17.

THE YOGA OF THREEFOLD DIVISION OF ŚRADDHĀ (DETERMINED FAITH)

17.1   Arjuna said: Those who worship, casting aside
the scriptural ordinance, endowed with śraddhā
(determined faith), what indeed is their state O
Krishna; sattva, rajas or tamas?

17.2   The blessed Lord said: Threefold is the śraddhā
(determined faith) born of individual nature of the
embodied: sāttvika, rājasika and tāmasika; listen to
it thus.

17.3   The śraddhā (determined faith) of everyone is in
accordance to one's nature, O Arjuna. A man is
made up of this faith; he is verily what his faith is.

17.4   The sāttvika worship the gods; rājasika the yakṣas
demigods and rākṣasas demons; the other people,
tāmasika worship the ghosts and host of spirits.

17.5   Those people who practice terrible austerity not
enjoined by the scripture, with much hypocrisy
and egoism, possessed by the power of lust and
attachment...

17.6   Torturing the elements in the body and even Me
embodied within, senseless, know them to be of
demoniac resolves.

17.7   Verily, the food dear to all also is threefold, as also
sacrifice, austerity and gift. Do hear this, their
distinction.

17.8   Foods which increase longevity, purity, strength,
health, joy and cheer, which are savory and rich

in oil, substantial and agreeable, are dear to the sāttvika.

17.9 Foods bitter, sour, salty, very hot, pungent, dry and burning, which produce pain, grief and disease, are relished by the rājasika.

17.10 Food that is stale, tasteless, putrid and rotten, also refuse and impure, is dear to the tāmasika.

17.11 The sacrifice offered by those desiring no fruit, as enjoined by ordinance, with the mind well resolved that they should merely sacrifice, that is sāttvika.

17.12 That sacrifice offered seeking indeed not only fruit but ostentation as well, know it to be rājasika O Arjuna.

17.13 Sacrifice which is severed from ordinance, in which no food is distributed, which is devoid of mantra holy words of power, gift and śraddhā (determined faith) is declared tāmasika.

17.14 *The worship of gods, twice-born, gurus and the wise and purity, uprightness, non-attachment and non-injury are called austerity of body.*

17.15 *The speech without excitement, which is truthful, pleasant and beneficial and also the practice of sacred study are called austerity of speech.*

17.16 *Serenity of mind, gentleness, silence, self-restraint and very pure disposition are called austerity of mind.*

17.17 That threefold austerity, practiced by devout men
with utmost, determined faith, and desiring no
fruit is declared sāttvika.

17.18 The austerity practiced with the object of gaining
reverence, honour and worship here and also with
ostentation is said to be rājasika, unstable and
transitory.

17.19 The austerity practiced with foolish notion,
torturing oneself or aiming to destroy another is
declared tāmasika.

17.20 *Gift given as obligatory, to a recipient who does
no service, and in place and in time, that gift is
considered sāttvika.*

17.21 *That gift given only to receive in return or expecting
a fruit, again reluctantly, is considered rājasika.*

17.22 *Gift given at a wrong place and time to unworthy
recipients, without respect, with insult, that is
declared tāmasika.*

17.23 Om Tat Sat (God, Reality, Truth) has been
considered the threefold designation of Brahman,
from which arose brāhmaṇas, Vedas and sacrifices
of yore.

17.24 Therefore, acts of sacrifice, gift and austerity, as
enjoined in the scriptures, are begun by students
of Brahman always uttering Om (God).

17.25 Without aiming at fruit, various acts of sacrifice, austerity and gift are performed by seekers for liberation — Tat (Reality).

17.26 Sat (Truth) — this is used in the sense of Reality and goodness, O Arjuna, also the word Sat is used as an auspicious act.

17.27 Steadfastness in sacrifice, austerity and gift is also called Sat, also action for Tat (Brahman) is even called Sat.

17.28 Whatever is sacrificed, given or done and whatever austerity is practiced without śraddhā (determined faith) is called asat (false), which is naught here or hereafter, O Arjuna.

18.

THE YOGA OF LIBERATION THROUGH RENUNCIATION

18.1　Arjuna said: I wish to know distinctly O Krishna, the truth of sannyāsa (renunciation), O Krishna, and of tyāga (relinquishment), O Krishna.

18.2　*The blessed Lord said: Sages understand sannyāsa to be renunciation of desire-ridden action; the relinquishment of fruit of all action, the wise declare as tyāga.*

18.3　Some philosophers declare thus action should be relinquished as evil; others (declare) that acts of sacrifice, gift, and austerity should not be relinquished.

18.4　Hear from Me clearly on tyāga (relinquishment) O Arjuna; tyāga verily has been declared to be threefold.

18.5　*The act of sacrifice, gift, and austerity should not be relinquished, that indeed should be performed; sacrifice, gift, and austerity are indeed purifiers of the wise.*

18.6　*But even these actions should be performed; relinquishing attachment and fruit is My firm and highest conviction.*

18.7　Verily, renunciation of obligatory action is not proper; tyāga (relinquishment) of that from delusion is declared tāmasika.

18.8　Indeed, he who relinquishes action that is painful, from fear of bodily trouble, thus performing

rājasika tyāga relinquishment, he does not obtain
the fruit of relinquishment.

18.9   *Whatever obligatory action which ought to be
        done, indeed performed, O Arjuna, relinquishing
        attachment and also fruit, that is regarded as
        sāttvika tyāga relinquishment.*

18.10   The tyāgī relinquisher does not hate disagreeable
        action, nor is he attached to agreeable one, being
        pervaded by sattva purity, intelligent, and his
        doubts cut asunder.

18.11   Verily, it is not possible for the embodied to
        relinquish actions totally, but he who relinquishes
        fruit of action is called a tyāgī.

18.12   The threefold desirable, undesirable, and mixed
        fruit of action accrues to non-relinquishers (atyāgī)
        but never to renunciates (sannyāsīs).

18.13   These five causes for accomplishment of all
        actions, learn from Me, O Arjuna, as declared in
        Sāṅkhya, which is the end of action.

18.14   The seat (body), doer, distinct types of instruments,
        distinct and various functions and also Lord, the
        fifth here.

18.15   Whatever action a man performs by body, speech
        and mind, whether right or otherwise, these five
        are its causes.

18.16   Such being the case, verily he who due to undeveloped intellect sees the Self alone as doer, he of imperfect judgment sees not.

18.17   Free from egoistic notion, he whose intellect is not tainted, even by killing these people he kills not, is not bound.

18.18   Knowledge, known, and knower are the threefold impulses to action; while instrument, action, and actor are the threefold constituents of action.

18.19   Knowledge, action, and actor are also said to be threefold according to the distinction in guṇas (qualities) in the science of guṇas; hear them also duly.

18.20   That by which one sees the one indestructible Being in all beings, inseparate in the separate, know that knowledge to be sāttvika (pure).

18.21   But that knowledge which by differentiation sees distinction and variety in all beings, know that knowledge to be rājasika (impure).

18.22   Indeed that which clings to a single facet as if the whole, without reason, without foundation in truth and is trivial, that is declared tāmasika (ignorant).

18.23   An obligatory action, executed without attachment, free from like or dislike and not desirous of fruit is called sāttvika (pure).

18.24 But action done by one longing for desired object or with egoism, again with much effort is declared rājasika (impure).

18.25 An action undertaken from delusion, regardless of the consequence, loss, injury and ability is called tāmasika (ignorant).

18.26 An actor free from attachment, not egoistic, endued with firmness and enthusiasm, unaffected by success and failure is called sāttvika (pure).

18.27 An actor who is passionate, desirous of fruit of action, greedy, cruel, tainted, moved by joy or sorrow is called rājasika (impure).

18.28 An actor who is not steadfast, is vulgar, stubborn, deceptive, malicious, lazy, despondent and procrastinating is called tāmasika (ignorant).

18.29 The threefold division of intellect and steadfastness according to guṇas (qualities) related fully and distinctly, do listen, O Arjuna.

18.30 The intellect which knows activity and renunciation, what ought to be done and what ought not, fear and fearlessness, bondage and liberation, that O Arjuna is sāttvika (pure).

18.31 The intellect which understands wrongly dharma (righteousness) and adharma (unrighteousness) and also what ought to be done and what ought not to be done, that O Arjuna is rājasika (impure).

18.32   The intellect enveloped in darkness which
        regards adharma (unrighteousness) as dharma
        (righteousness) and all things perverted, that O
        Arjuna is tāmasika (ignorant).

18.33   The steadfastness with which one holds the
        activities of the mind, prāṇa (life-breath),
        and senses, unswerving through yoga — that
        steadfastness, O Arjuna, is sāttvika (pure).

18.34   But the steadfastness with which one clings
        to duty, pleasure, and wealth, O Arjuna, much
        attached and desirous of fruit, that steadfastness,
        O Arjuna, is rājasika (impure).

18.35   The steadfastness with which a fool indeed does
        not give up dreaming, fear, grief, despair and
        arrogance, that, O Arjuna, is tāmasika (impure).

18.36   And now hear indeed from Me O Arjuna, the
        threefold happiness where one by practice rejoices
        and ends sorrow.

18.37   What is like poison in the beginning and nectar in
        the end, that happiness is declared sāttvika (pure),
        a blessing born from clarity of one's intellect.

18.38   The happiness arising from contact of sense-organ
        with object, which in the beginning is like nectar
        and in the end like poison, that is considered
        rājasika (impure).

18.39   The happiness delusive of Self in the beginning and in the sequel, arising from sleep, indolence, and heedlessness, that is said to be tāmasika (ignorant).

18.40   There is no being on earth, nor even in heaven among the gods, who is free from these three guṇas (qualities), born of prakṛti (matter).

18.41   The actions of brāhmaṇas, kṣatriyas, vaiśyas and śūdras, O Arjuna, are well classified by guṇas (qualities) born of their nature.

18.42   Serenity, self-restraint, austerity, purity, forgiveness, uprightness, also knowledge, wisdom and determined faith are characteristic of brāhmaṇa (the priest-class), born of their nature.

18.43   Prowess, splendour, steadfastness, dexterity and also not fleeing from battle, charity and lordliness are characteristic of kṣatriya (warrior-class), born of their nature.

18.44   Agriculture, cattle-rearing, trade are characteristic of vaiśya (merchant, trader, and farmer-class), born of their nature and service-orientation is the characteristic of śūdra (laborer), born of their nature.

18.45   Devoted each to their characteristic, they attain complete fulfillment; how one engaged in one's action attains fulfillment, that do listen.

18.46 Worshiping Him, with one's action, from Whom
beings emerge, by Whom all this is pervaded, one
attains perfection.

18.47 Better is svadharma (one's duty), though without
merit, than paradharma (duty of another) well
performed; *performing action ordained by one's
nature one incurs no sin (agitation).*

18.48 The action born with oneself, O Arjuna,
though faulty, one should not relinquish for all
undertakings are fault-ridden, as fire by smoke.

18.49 He whose intellect is not attached anywhere,
conquered their self, liberated from desire, they
attain the supreme perfection of actionlessness
through renunciation.

18.50 Also learn from Me briefly, O Arjuna, how one who
has attained perfection reaches Brahman, that
supreme consummation of Knowledge.

18.51 Endued with a very pure intellect, having
controlled self through firmness, relinquished
sound and other sense objects, renounced love
and hatred and...

18.52 Living without need of company, eating but a
little, with speech, body and mind controlled,
ever engaged in yoga of meditation, endued with
dispassion...

18.53   Freed from egoism, power, arrogance, desire,
        anger, covetousness, mineness; being peaceful,
        one is fit for becoming Brahman.

18.54   Becoming Brahman, serene in Self, he neither
        grieves nor desires; alike to all beings, he attains
        supreme devotion to Me.

18.55   By devotion, he knows Me in essence — what
        and who I am. Then knowing Me in essence, he
        forthwith enters into That.

18.56   Performing all actions always taking refuge
        in Me, by My grace, one reaches the eternal,
        indestructible Abode.

18.57   Consciously resigning all actions unto Me,
        regarding Me as supreme, resorting to yoga of
        discrimination, fix your mind ever on Me.

18.58   Fixing the mind on Me, you shall by My grace
        overcome all obstacles. If from egoism, you will not
        listen, you shall perish.

18.59   If out of egoism, you resolve 'I will not fight' — vain
        is this resolve of yours. Your nature will constrain
        you.

18.60   Bound by action born of your nature, O Arjuna,
        that which from delusion, you do not like to do,
        even that, helplessly, you will perform.

18.61   The Lord dwells in the hearts of all beings, O
        Arjuna, causing by māyā (illusive nature) all beings
        to revolve, (as if) mounted on a machine.

18.62   Seek refuge in Him alone, with all your being, O
        Arjuna; by His grace, you shall attain supreme
        peace, the eternal Abode.

18.63   Thus, knowledge most secret has been declared to
        you by Me, having reflected on this fully, act as you
        will.

18.64   Hear again My supreme word, the most secret of
        all — you are dear to Me, so I will speak what is
        good for you.

18.65   Fix the mind on Me, be devoted to Me, sacrifice
        to Me, bow down to Me. Truly, I promise you shall
        come to Me alone, you are dear to Me.

18.66   Relinquishing fully all dharmas (natures), take
        refuge in Me alone, I will liberate you from all sins
        (agitations), grieve not.

18.67   This is not to be spoken by you to one devoid of
        austerity, not devoted, does not render service, or
        speaks ill of Me.

18.68   He who shall teach this supreme secret to My
        devotees, having shown the greatest devotion to
        Me alone, shall doubtless come to Me.

18.69   There is none among men who does dearer service
        to Me than he, nor shall there be another in the
        world dearer to Me than them.

18.70   And they who shall study this sacred dialogue
        of ours, by them I am worshiped by jñāna yajña
        (sacrifice of wisdom); such is My view.

18.71 And even the man who listens, imbued with
śraddhā (determined faith), free from malice and
liberated — they too shall attain the worlds of
those of meritorious deeds.

18.72 Has this been heard by you with single-pointed
mind, O Arjuna? Has the deep delusion of
ignorance been destroyed, O Arjuna?

18.73 Arjuna said: My delusion is cleared and
understanding restored by your grace, O Krishna.
I am firm. With doubt dispelled, I will do your
bidding.

18.74 Sañjaya said: Thus have I heard this wonderful
dialogue between enlightened Krishna and Arjuna,
which makes the hair stand on end.

18.75 By the grace of Vyāsa have I heard this secret, the
supreme yoga declared directly by the Lord of
yoga, Krishna, Himself.

18.76 O king, remembering again and again this
wonderful and holy dialogue between Krishna and
Arjuna, I rejoice again and again.

18.77 And remembering again and again that most
wonderful form of Hari (god of preservation), great
is my wonder O king, and I rejoice again and again.

18.78 Wherever Krishna, the Lord of yoga, is and Arjuna,
the archer, arises prosperity, victory, glory, and
sound policy; that is my conviction.

-End-

This version of the Gita originates from the translation
of A. Parthasarathy, with the multitudes of nicknames
for both Krishna and Arjuna removed for legibility,
along with additional amendments and parentheticals
for context, grammar, and punctuation for the same
purpose. The original A. Parthasarathy version,
along with online recorded lectures of his found at
-vedantaworld.org- is the graduation from this version
for interpretation, explanation, and reflection from all
angles, all from the perspective of a realized Being (and
in plain English). This final point cannot be overstated.